MW00441172

THE LITTLE
BOOK
ABOUT
HEAVEN

ron rhodes

HARVEST HOUSE PUBLISHERS
EUGENE, OREGON

THE LITTLE BOOK ABOUT HEAVEN
Copyright © 2013 by Ron Rhodes
Published by Harvest House Publishers
Eugene, Oregon 97402
www.harvesthousepublishers.com

ISBN 978-0-7369-5183-8 (hardcover)
ISBN 978-0-7369-5184-5 (eBook)

Printed in China

13 14 15 16 17 18 19 20 21 / FC-JH / 10 9 8 7 6 5 4 3 2 1

Contents

Thank you for your interest in this book! I pray that even though it is a little book, it will bring a big blessing to your life. It is uniquely formatted...

▶ Each chapter is short—just two pages.

▶ Each chapter begins by stating the big idea.

▶ This is followed by bullet points that concisely expand on the big idea, with Bible references.

▶ I then quote a few of the very best Bible verses that illustrate the big idea.

▶ On the second page of each chapter, I provide "fast facts" that relate to the big idea.

▶ Each chapter closes with some applications— "truths that transform"—and a thoughtful quote from a recent or not-so-recent Christian leader.

This abbreviated format allows for maximum information in minimal space. This is a little book, but it contains lots of information. Feel free to look up some of the verses I cite. That will greatly enrich your study.

Here's an added benefit of the book. Because it contains 28 chapters, it is ideally suited for four weeks of brief daily devotionals on the doctrine of heaven.

The Gold Color of This Book

The gold color of this little book is significant. It reflects the teaching of the book of Revelation that the New Jerusalem—the heavenly eternal city in which Christians will live forever—is "pure gold, like clear glass...pure gold, like transparent glass" (21:18,21).

Illumination Through Prayer

I suggest that you begin each chapter with a short prayer. Ask God to open your spiritual eyes of understanding so that you can fully grasp what He wants you to understand. The psalmist set a great example for us. He prayed, "Open my eyes, that I may behold wondrous things out of your law" (Psalm 119:18). The Holy Spirit delights in illumining our minds to spiritual truths (1 Corinthians 2:10-11).

Anticipate Spiritual Blessing

As you learn more about heaven, expect to be blessed spiritually. Remember that Bible study is not just about head apprehension, it's also about life-transforming heart appropriation (see Romans 12:2). Of course, we must willingly submit ourselves to Scripture for this to occur. As Scripture puts it, we must be doers of the Word, and not just hearers (James 1:22). Doers of the Word experience the blessings of the Word (Psalm 1)!

There Are Three Heavens

THE BIG IDEA

Scripture addresses three different heavens.

What You Need to Know

- ▶ God created all three heavens (Genesis 1:1).

- ▶ The first heaven is the earth's atmosphere (Genesis 1:20; 8:2; Psalm 147:8; Matthew 8:20).

- ▶ The second heaven is the stellar universe, brimming with planets, stars, and galaxies (Genesis 1:14-15,17; 15:5; Deuteronomy 4:19).

- ▶ The third heaven is the ineffable and glorious dwelling place of God in all of His glory (2 Corinthians 12:2). It is the "highest heaven" (1 Kings 8:27; 2 Chronicles 2:6).

Verses to Contemplate

"The LORD looks down from heaven on the children of man, to see if there are any who understand, who seek after God" (Psalm 14:2).

"Our Father in heaven, hallowed be your name. Your

kingdom come, your will be done, on earth as it is in heaven" (Matthew 6:9-10).

Truths That Transform

1. Observing the majesty of the first and second heavens gives us a glimpse of God's awesome glory (Psalm 19:1).
2. We are sojourners on the earth, but we ought to keep our vision focused on the things of the third heaven (Colossians 3:1-2).
3. Our future life there ought to influence our present life here (1 Peter 2:11).
4. Let's be heavenly-minded Christians.

A Quote to Ponder

"The lack of long, strong thinking about our promised hope of glory is a major cause of our plodding, lack-luster lifestyle...It is the heavenly Christian that is the lively Christian."

J.I. Packer

Life on Earth Is Short

THE BIG IDEA

Because life on earth is so short, it makes good sense to daily live in view of our eternal existence in heaven.

What You Need to Know

▶ Just as a puff of smoke quickly disperses in the air and disappears, so human life seems to vanish all too quickly (James 4:14).

▶ A glance at some old photographs shows that our youthful beauty is fading quickly and steadily (1 Peter 1:24).

▶ We may eat healthy foods and exercise vigorously, but we will still age and die, and this process happens far faster than we're comfortable with (Psalm 144:4).

Verses to Contemplate

"Behold, you have made my days a few handbreadths, and my lifetime is as nothing before you. Surely all mankind stands as a mere breath!" (Psalm 39:5).

"All flesh is like grass and all its glory like the flower of grass. The grass withers, and the flower falls" (1 Peter 1:24).

FAST FACTS
Life Is Like…

a mist that disperses (James 4:14)

grass or a flower that withers (1 Peter 1:24)

a shadow that passes (Psalm 144:4)

a wind that blows by (Psalm 78:39)

Truths That Transform

1. Out of all the eternal ages of our existence as the children of God, these few years on earth determine our destiny and can never be repeated.
2. It is therefore wisest to live in full commitment to the Lord every moment of every day (Matthew 6:19-21).
3. An awareness of our mortality instills in us a desire to make every day count (Psalm 39:4).

A Quote to Ponder

"Time is short. Eternity is long. It is only reasonable that this short life be lived in the light of eternity."

Charles Spurgeon

3

We All Experience Death

THE BIG IDEA

At the moment of death, the believer's spirit goes to heaven. The unbeliever's spirit goes to a place of confinement and punishment.

What You Need to Know

▶ At death, the soul (or spirit) departs from the material body (Genesis 35:18).

▶ Believers go to be with the Lord in heaven (2 Corinthians 5:8; Philippians 1:21-23).

▶ Unbelievers go to a place of temporary confinement (2 Peter 2:9) to await the future great white throne judgment and eternal punishment (Revelation 20:11-15).

Verses to Contemplate

At death "the spirit returns to God who gave it" (Ecclesiastes 12:7).

"As they were stoning Stephen, he called out, 'Lord Jesus, receive my spirit'" (Acts 7:59).

the way of all the earth (1 Kings 2:1-2)

the journey of no return (Job 16:22)

breathing one's last (Genesis 25:17)

a tent being destroyed (2 Corinthians 5:1-5)

Truths That Transform

1. The Bible talks about death so that it can instruct us about life (Psalm 90:12).
2. The Bible talks about death so that it can teach us how to have an eternal perspective.
3. The reality of impending death detaches our interest from the things of this temporal world, which is passing away, and centers our attention on the afterlife (Colossians 3:1-2).

A Quote to Ponder

"However big and pressing the questions related to our present short life on earth may seem, they shrink into littleness compared with this timeless, measureless concern of death and the vast hereafter. How long earthly life looks to questing youth! How quickly fled it seems to the aged!"

J. Sidlow Baxter

The Intermediate State Follows Death

THE BIG IDEA

The intermediate state relates to the time between the death of our mortal bodies and our future resurrection.

What You Need to Know

- ▶ At death, the Christian's spirit goes directly to heaven (2 Corinthians 5:8). Physical death is therefore a step into blissful joy (1 Corinthians 15:55) and is not to be feared.

- ▶ However, at death, the unbeliever's spirit is confined (2 Peter 2:9) and awaits eternal condemnation (Revelation 20:11-15).

Verses to Contemplate

"We would rather be away from the body and at home with the Lord" (2 Corinthians 5:8).

"My desire is to depart and be with Christ, for that is far better" (Philippians 1:23).

Believers are in conscious bliss (Philippians 1:23).

Unbelievers are in conscious woe (Mark 9:43-48).

Jesus said that Lazarus, the rich man, and Abraham were all conscious (Luke 16:19-31).

The souls of martyrs cry out (Revelation 6:9-10).

Old Testament saints are living (Luke 20:38).

Truths That Transform

1. When we depart the body to be with Christ in heaven, we are released from earthly hardships and heartaches.
2. We will be in paradise—a term meaning "garden of pleasure" (Luke 23:43; 2 Corinthians 12:2-3).
3. What lies beyond the grave for the Christian is incomprehensively awesome (1 Corinthians 2:9).

A Quote to Ponder

"Resolved, that I will live so as I shall wish I had done when I come to die...Resolved, to endeavor to my utmost to act as I can think I should do, if I had already seen the happiness of heaven, and hell's torments."

Jonathan Edwards

The Rapture Is Imminent

THE BIG IDEA

At the rapture (before the future tribulation period), believers who are living as well as those who have died will be caught up to meet Christ in the air (1 Corinthians 15:51-52; 1 Thessalonians 4:13-17).

What You Need to Know

▶ Christians who have died and those who are still alive will receive resurrection bodies that are imperishable and immortal (1 Corinthians 15:53).

▶ They will then be taken back to heaven, never again to be separated from Christ (John 14:1-3; 1 Thessalonians 4:13-17).

▶ The event is imminent (see Romans 13:11-12; James 5:7-9).

Verses to Contemplate

"The dead in Christ will rise first. Then we who are alive, who are left, will be caught up together with them in the clouds to meet the Lord in the air, and so we will always be with the Lord" (1 Thessalonians 4:16-17).

At the Rapture	At the Second Coming
Christ comes *for* the saints.	Christ comes *with* the saints.
We meet Christ in the air.	Christ comes to the earth.
Christ leads us back to heaven.	Christ remains on earth.
The tribulation has not begun.	The tribulation has ended.

Truths That Transform

1. Christ is the divine Bridegroom (John 3:29), and the church is the bride of Christ (Revelation 19:7).

2. At the rapture, Christ will come to claim His bride (the church) and take her to the Father's house (heaven), where He has prepared a place for her (John 14:1-3).

3. Meanwhile, as the betrothed bride awaits her Groom, she seeks to live in purity, fidelity, and faithfulness (Romans 13:11-14; 2 Peter 3:10-14).

A Quote to Ponder

"If the Lord is coming soon, is this not a very practical motive for greater missionary effort? I know of no other motive that has been so stimulating to myself."

J. Hudson Taylor

We Will All Receive Body Upgrades

THE BIG IDEA

Though our earthly bodies die, someday we will be physically resurrected with eternal bodies.

What You Need to Know

► Our mortal, perishable bodies will be resurrected immortal and imperishable (1 Corinthians 15:42-43).

► Our present bodies are like tents, but our resurrection bodies will be like buildings (2 Corinthians 5:1-8).

► Our resurrection bodies will be physical, like Christ's (see Luke 24:39; Philippians 3:21).

Verses to Contemplate

"I am the resurrection and the life. Whoever believes in me, though he die, yet shall he live" (John 11:25).

"When the perishable puts on the imperishable, and the mortal puts on immortality, then shall come to pass the saying that is written: 'Death is swallowed up in victory'" (1 Corinthians 15:54).

FAST FACTS
Contrasts in 1 Corinthians 15:43,53

The Earthly Body	The Resurrection Body
perishable	imperishable
dies in dishonor	raised in glory
dies in weakness	raised in power

Truths That Transform

1. Our present bodies are like tents—temporary, flimsy, and fragile (2 Corinthians 5:1-2).
2. Our resurrection bodies will be like buildings—permanent, sturdy, and strong.
3. Every time we look in a mirror, our temporary tents remind us that eternity is rapidly approaching (2 Corinthians 4:16).
4. Aging helps us develop an eternal perspective (Psalm 90:12; Colossians 3:1-2).

A Quote to Ponder

"I still can hardly believe it. I, with shriveled, bent fingers, atrophied muscles, gnarled knees, and no feeling from the shoulders down, will one day have a new body, light, bright, and clothed in righteousness—powerful and dazzling."

Joni Eareckson Tada

We Will All Face Judgment

THE BIG IDEA

All believers will one day stand before the judgment seat of Christ (the *Bema*).

What You Need to Know

▶ This judgment has nothing to do with whether the Christian will remain saved (John 10:28-30; Romans 8:29-39). It has to do with the reception or loss of rewards, based on how we lived.

▶ This judgment will focus on our actions (Psalm 62:12; Matthew 16:27; Ephesians 6:7-8), thoughts (Jeremiah 17:10; 1 Corinthians 4:5; Revelation 2:23), and words (Matthew 12:35-37).

Verses to Contemplate

"We will all stand before the judgment seat of God" (Romans 14:10).

"We must all appear before the judgment seat of Christ, so that each one may receive what is due for what he has done in the body, whether good or evil" (2 Corinthians 5:10).

The crown of life is for those who persevere (James 1:12).

The crown of glory is for those who minister God's Word (1 Peter 5:4).

The crown incorruptible is for those who maintain self-control (1 Corinthians 9:25).

The crown of righteousness is for those who long for the second coming (2 Timothy 4:8).

Truths That Transform

1. The greater our rewards in heaven, the greater will be our capacity to bring glory to God in the afterlife (1 Corinthians 3:10-15; Revelation 4:10-11).

2. Conversely, the lesser our rewards in heaven, the lesser will be our capacity to glorify God in the afterlife.

3. Is this not a powerful motivation for faithful service to the Lord?

A Quote to Ponder

*"O spend your time as you would
hear of it in the Judgment!"*
Richard Baxter

Heaven Is a Physical Place

THE BIG IDEA

Heaven will be not an ethereal spiritual dimension but rather a physical place.

What You Need to Know

▶ Heaven—including the new heavens and the new earth—must be a physical place, for you and I will have physically resurrected bodies (1 Corinthians 15:35-53; see also Luke 24:39).

▶ Physical bodies require a physical dwelling place. A physical resurrection makes no sense apart from a physical heaven (see John 14:1-2).

▶ Revelation 21:9–22:5 describes heaven as a physical place—it is a city with walls, gates, foundations, a street, river, trees, and more.

Verses to Contemplate

"In my Father's house are many rooms...I go to prepare a place for you" (John 14:2).

Heaven is "the city that has foundations, whose designer and builder is God" (Hebrews 11:10).

Heaven is "a better country, that is, a heavenly one" (Hebrews 11:16).

FAST FACTS
Christ, the Designer-Creator

Christ designed and created the stellar universe (John 1:3; Colossians 1:16; Hebrews 1:2).

Christ is also designing and creating our heavenly home, the New Jerusalem (John 14:1-3).

Truths That Transform

1. You and I will have physically resurrected bodies and live in a physical city (the new Jerusalem) on a physical earth (the new earth) in a physical universe (the new heavens).
2. Let this awe-inspiring reality saturate your daily mindset.

A Quote to Ponder

"Paradise was not generally understood [in Bible times] as mere allegory, with a metaphorical or spiritual meaning, but as an actual physical place where God and his people lived together, surrounded by physical beauty, enjoying great pleasures and happiness."

Randy Alcorn

Heaven Has a Real Location

THE BIG IDEA

Christians have different ideas as to where heaven is located, and each has some merit.

What You Need to Know

▶ Some believe heaven is in the north of the universe, shrouded by a cloud of God's glory (see Job 26:7; 37:22; Isaiah 14:13-14).

▶ Others note that heaven can apparently be "torn open" in the sky (Mark 1:10). Perhaps Jesus, after His resurrection, appeared from this dimension to His disciples (Luke 24:31; John 20:26).

▶ Whichever view one holds to, heaven transcends anything the human mind can imagine (1 Corinthians 2:9).

Verses to Contemplate

The apostle Paul "was caught up to the third heaven" (2 Corinthians 12:2-4).

"For thus says the One who is high and lifted up, who

inhabits eternity, whose name is Holy: I dwell in the high and holy place" (Isaiah 57:15).

Truths That Transform

1. The most important thing about heaven's location is that God dwells there (Psalm 68:5).
2. The psalmist prays, "In your presence there is fullness of joy; at your right hand are pleasures forevermore" (Psalm 16:11).
3. Regardless of where heaven is, we will blissfully live in God's direct presence (Revelation 21:3).

A Quote to Ponder

"[Heaven] is a real place where people with physical bodies will dwell in God's presence for all eternity; and it is also a realm that surpasses our finite concept of what a 'place' is."

John MacArthur

Heaven Is Paradise

THE BIG IDEA

Paradise was lost by our first parents (Adam and Eve), but paradise will one day be restored.

What You Need to Know

- ▶ The word "paradise" means "garden of pleasure" or "garden of delight."

- ▶ Paradise is a place of incredible bliss in the very presence of God (1 Corinthians 2:9).

- ▶ Revelation 2:7 refers to heaven as the "paradise of God."

- ▶ The apostle Paul "was caught up into paradise" and "heard things that cannot be told, which man may not utter" (2 Corinthians 12:3-4). It must be awesome!

- ▶ Paul wanted to go back (Philippians 1:23).

Verses to Contemplate

"Truly, I say to you, today you will be with me in Paradise" (Luke 23:43).

"To the one who conquers I will grant to eat of the tree of life, which is in the paradise of God" (Revelation 2:7).

FAST FACTS

Paradise Lost	Paradise Regained
lost by Adam and Eve	restored to Christians
in the Garden of Eden	in heaven
sin and death began	sin and death are gone forever
tree of life is barred	tree of life is restored
book of Genesis	book of Revelation

Truths That Transform

1. Paradise is the seat and dwelling place of the divine Majesty (Revelation 2:7).
2. Our beloved Lord's presence in paradise makes it wonderful (Revelation 21:1-4).
3. There is no waiting period following death. Jesus told the thief, "Today you will be with me in Paradise" (Luke 23:43).
4. Meditate on these blessed realities!

A Quote to Ponder

"This world is the land of the dying; the next is the land of the living."

Tryon Edwards

11

A Heavenly Country Awaits Us

THE BIG IDEA

Believers are sojourning on earth but are seeking a better country—a wondrous heavenly country.

What You Need to Know

▶ The great warriors of the faith in biblical times were not satisfied with earthly, temporal things. That is why they sought an eternal heavenly country (Hebrews 11:13-16).

▶ The word "country" is used as a metaphor of heaven. The heavenly country is unlike earthly countries. There is no sorrow or suffering there.

Verses to Contemplate

"They desire a better country, that is, a heavenly one. Therefore God is not ashamed to be called their God, for he has prepared for them a city" (Hebrews 11:16).

"You have come to Mount Zion and to the city of the living God, the heavenly Jerusalem" (Hebrews 12:22).

Peter called Christians "elect exiles" on the earth
(1 Peter 1:1).

He also referred to them as "sojourners and exiles"
(1 Peter 2:11).

The faithful are "strangers and exiles" (Hebrews 11:13).

Truths That Transform

1. You and I are pilgrims making our way to the heavenly country (Hebrews 11:16).
2. Sometimes our journey can be grueling, at times exhausting (Romans 5:3).
3. The good news is that the trials of our earthly pilgrimage pale in the face of the glories of the heavenly country (Romans 8:17-18).
4. Take comfort in this realization!

A Quote to Ponder

"The heavenly country is full of light and glory; having the delightful breezes of divine love, and the comfortable gales of the blessed Spirit...Here is a freedom from a body subject to diseases and death, from a body of sin and death, from Satan's temptations, from all doubts, fears, and unbelief, and from all sorrows and afflictions."

John Gill

Heaven Has Many Occupants

THE BIG IDEA

Heaven is inhabited by the triune God, angels, and believers of all ages.

What You Need to Know

- ▶ Heaven is God's habitat. His throne is in heaven, and He reigns from there (Acts 7:49).

- ▶ At the same time, God is omnipresent (everywhere-present) (Psalm 139:7-12).

- ▶ Angels live in heaven, though they go on assignments outside of heaven (Daniel 9:21).

- ▶ Redeemed human beings will spend all eternity in heaven, fellowshipping with God and the angels (John 14:1-3; Philippians 3:20).

Verses to Contemplate

God is in heaven. "The LORD has established his throne in the heavens" (Psalm 103:19).

Angels are in heaven. "I saw the LORD sitting on his throne, and all the host of heaven standing on his right hand and on his left" (2 Chronicles 18:18).

Human beings are in heaven. Believers will forever enjoy "a better country, that is, a heavenly one" (Hebrews 11:16).

Truths That Transform

1. One of the joys of heaven is that we'll be face-to-face with God (Revelation 21:3).
2. Another joy is that we'll be reunited with Christian loved ones (1 Thessalonians 4:13-17).
3. We'll also join with the angels in worship of our wondrous God (Revelation 7:9-12).
4. Let these truths penetrate deep into your soul.

A Quote to Ponder

"For Christians, death on its earthward side is simply that the tired mortal body falls temporarily to sleep, while on the heavenward side we suddenly find ourselves with our dear Savior-King and with other Christian loved ones in the heavenly home. Why fear that?"

J. Sidlow Baxter

We Will Enjoy a Glorious Reunion

THE BIG IDEA

In heaven we will enjoy a never-ending reunion with all our Christian loved ones.

What You Need to Know

▶ The future rapture of the church is called a "blessed hope" (Titus 2:13). One aspect of this blessedness is our eternal reunion with Christian loved ones.

▶ Paul comforted the Thessalonian Christians by telling them they'd be reunited with their deceased Christian loved ones (1 Thessalonians 4:13-18).

▶ David likewise looked forward to an afterlife reunion with his deceased son (2 Samuel 12:23; see also Matthew 8:11; Luke 16:19-31; 20:38).

Verses to Contemplate

"The dead in Christ will rise first. Then we who are alive, who are left, will be caught up together with them in the clouds to meet the Lord in the air, and so we will always be with the Lord. Therefore encourage one another with these words" (1 Thessalonians 4:16-18).

At the moment of death, the believer is "gathered to his people" (Genesis 25:17; 35:29; 49:33; Judges 2:10).

FAST FACTS
We Will Recognize Each Other in the Afterlife

Lazarus, the rich man, and Abraham recognized each other (Luke 16:19-31).

Many will recline at a table with Abraham, Isaac, and Jacob (Matthew 8:11).

Truths That Transform

1. Our reunion in heaven will be especially sweet because none of us will have sin natures (Philippians 3:21). We will have no quarrels, resentments, jealousies, or rivalries; no one-upmanship, cross words, or misunderstandings.
2. Our relationships in heaven will truly be wonderful and utterly satisfying.

A Quote to Ponder

"Our pleasant communion with our kind Christian friends is only broken off for a small moment, and is soon to be eternally resumed...Blessed and happy indeed will that meeting be—better a thousand times than the parting! We parted in sorrow, and we shall meet in joy."

J.C. Ryle

We Will Enjoy Communion with God

THE BIG IDEA

Christians will enjoy unbroken and unfettered fellowship with God for all eternity.

What You Need to Know

▶ Nothing can be more sublime and utterly satisfying for Christians than unbroken fellowship with God (John 14:3; 2 Corinthians 5:6-8; Philippians 1:23; 1 Thessalonians 4:17).

▶ The crowning wonder of our experience in heaven will be the perpetual and endless exploration of the glory of God Himself (Revelation 21:3; 22:4).

▶ No wonder the psalmist exulted, "You will fill me with joy in your presence, with eternal pleasures at your right hand" (Psalm 16:11 NIV).

Verses to Contemplate

"The dwelling place of God is with man. He will dwell with them, and they will be his people, and God himself will be with them as their God" (Revelation 21:3).

"They will see his face" (Revelation 22:4).

Truths That Transform

1. When our beloved Christ was born on earth, He was called Immanuel, which means "God with us" (Matthew 1:23).

2. In the afterlife, Jesus will be with us in the closest possible sense—"face to face" (1 Corinthians 13:12; Revelation 22:4).

3. Our close intimacy will never be broken.

4. Can you get into an "Immanuel" state of mind as you think about heaven?

A Quote to Ponder

"God will dwell among His cleansed people, and they will experience intimate fellowship with Him. This is the supreme blessing of the New Jerusalem."

Thomas Constable

We Will Enjoy Communion with Angels

THE BIG IDEA

In addition to fellowshipping with God and with Christian loved ones in heaven, believers will also fellowship with the angels—and have authority over them.

What You Need to Know

- ▶ Angels escort us to heaven at death (Luke 16:22).
- ▶ When we enter into glory, we will be able to perceive angels as clearly as we perceive one another here on earth (1 Corinthians 13:12).
- ▶ We will jointly serve and worship our glorious King, Jesus Christ, from age to age forevermore (Revelation 7:9-12).
- ▶ Redeemed humans will also judge and exercise authority over the angels (1 Corinthians 6:3).

Verses to Contemplate

"Before me was a great multitude that no one could count, from every nation, tribe, people and language, standing before the throne and before the Lamb…All the angels were standing around the throne…They fell down on their faces before the throne and worshiped God" (Revelation 7:9,11 NIV).

FAST FACTS
The Nature of Angels

Angels are...

invisible (Hebrews 1:14)	holy (Psalm 89:7)
localized (Daniel 9:21-23)	obedient (Psalm 103:20)
powerful (Psalm 103:20)	immortal (Luke 20:36)

Truths That Transform

1. Thinking about angels reminds us that there's another world all around us—a spiritual world.
2. The angels already experience the fullness of that other world—God's wondrous and eternal heaven, where God Himself is encountered face-to-face.
3. A day is coming when you and I will experience the same (Revelation 21:1-4). Ponder that day!

A Quote to Ponder

"In heaven, those whose souls have been redeemed by the bloodshed of Christ will serve Him with gladness and will in turn be served by God's holy angels."

Billy Graham

We Will Eat Food in Heaven

THE BIG IDEA

We will be able to eat and enjoy food in our resurrection bodies.

What You Need to Know

▶ Jesus ate physical food four times after His resurrection from the dead (Luke 24:30,42-43; John 21:12-13; Acts 1:4).

▶ Our resurrection bodies will be like Jesus's resurrection body (Philippians 3:21; 1 John 3:2).

▶ Revelation 22:1-2 speaks of the fruit-bearing tree of life, from which the redeemed will apparently feast throughout eternity.

Verses to Contemplate

The disciples gave the resurrected Jesus "a piece of broiled fish, and he took it and ate before them" (Luke 24:42-43).

The tree of life in heaven bears "twelve kinds of fruit, yielding its fruit every month" (Revelation 22:1-2).

"The Lord Jesus Christ...will transform our lowly body to be like his glorious body" (Philippians 3:21).

"When he appears we shall be like him" (1 John 3:2).

"When Christ who is your life appears, then you also will appear with him in glory" (Colossians 3:4).

Truths That Transform

1. "No eye has seen, no ear has heard, and no mind has imagined what God has prepared for those who love him" (1 Corinthians 2:9 NLT).
2. This promise likely includes the reality that we'll be able to eat and enjoy food in the afterlife.
3. God is graciously making every provision for us to enjoy a truly abundant and fulfilled existence in the afterlife. Rejoice in this truth!

A Quote to Ponder

"Incredible gourmet delights will be enjoyed. This underscores the truth that God's design for us is that we may enjoy Him forever. Much of heaven is designed for sheer pleasure—both the pleasure of God and the pleasure of His people."

John MacArthur

Infants Who Die Are in Heaven

THE BIG IDEA

Infants and young children who die before maturing into a state of moral awareness go directly to heaven based on Christ's gracious atonement.

What You Need to Know

- ▶ Infants are born sinful (Ephesians 2:3), but they are not yet morally aware (James 4:17).

- ▶ If an infant dies before reaching moral awareness, the benefits of Christ's death are applied to the child, based on God's grace (Ephesians 1:7-8).

- ▶ God's wrath is only for those who willfully turn from Him (Romans 2:8).

- ▶ Infants and children are never mentioned in contexts of judgment or hell.

Verses to Contemplate

Christ's salvation is "according to the riches of his grace, which he lavished upon us, in all wisdom and insight" (Ephesians 1:7-8).

King David affirmed of his dead son, "I shall go to him, but he will not return to me" (2 Samuel 12:23).

Truths That Transform

1. Jesus loves little children. They are the special objects of His tender affection (Matthew 18:1-6).
2. Jesus even said we must become like children to enter His kingdom (Matthew 18:3).
3. Infants who have died are surely resting in the sweetness of His infinite love (2 Samuel 12:23).
4. If you or someone you know has experienced the loss of a child, meditate on these comforting truths of Scripture.

A Quote to Ponder

"God does not abandon the tiny ones...He has a plan for those too young to believe. A place has been made in heaven, safe in the arms of Jesus."
Robert Lightner

18

Our Pets Might Be in Heaven

THE BIG IDEA

It is entirely possible that God's redemptive purposes include the animal kingdom.

What You Need to Know

▶ Some theologians say that even though animals are not created in God's image (Genesis 1:26), they may have souls. Thus, nothing in Scripture precludes the possibility of animals' continued existence in the afterlife.

▶ Redemption is portrayed in cosmic terms. Romans 8:21 tells us that creation itself is destined to be redeemed through Christ.

▶ Animals are part of the creation, so they may be included in God's redemptive purposes. Recall that God saved the animals from the flood (Genesis 6:19-20).

Verses to Contemplate

"The creation looks forward to the day when it will join

God's children in glorious freedom from death and decay" (Romans 8:21 NLT).

Peter referred to "the time for restoring all the things about which God spoke" (Acts 3:21).

Truths That Transform

1. Psalm 148 refers to all of creation rendering praise to God, including great sea creatures, livestock, things that creep, and birds (see also Psalm 150:6).
2. If it is true that our animals will be in the afterlife, then they will render praise and worship to God along with the rest of creation.

A Quote to Ponder

"Revelation tells us that heaven will contain many of the same things that were in the original creation, such as a river, trees, and fruit. Why not animals too?"

Mark Hitchcock

There Is Time in Eternal Heaven

THE BIG IDEA

Those in eternal heaven continue to sense the passing of time.

What You Need to Know

▶ We will sing in heaven (Revelation 5:9; 14:3; 15:3). Songs with a beat and lyrics require a sense of moments passing.

▶ Revelation 6:10 (NIV) portrays martyred believers in heaven asking God, "How long, Sovereign Lord… until you judge the inhabitants of the earth and avenge our blood?"

▶ There is "silence in heaven for about half an hour" after the opening of the seventh seal (Revelation 8:1).

▶ Those who reside in heaven rejoice whenever a sinner repents on temporal earth (Luke 15:7).

Verses to Contemplate

"They are before the throne of God, and serve him day and night" (Revelation 7:15).

The tree of life is described as "yielding its fruit each month" (Revelation 22:1-2).

FAST FACTS
Proper Use of Time While Yet on Earth

Our times are in God's hands (Psalm 31:15).

Trust God at all times (Psalm 62:8).

Do good at all times (Psalm 106:3).

The time we have is subject to God (James 4:13-17).

Truths That Transform

1. God transcends time, so He can see the past, present, and future as a single intuitive act.
2. The past, present, and future are all encompassed in one ever-present "now" to Him.
3. Yet God can still act within time. God is eternal, but He can do temporal things. His acts take place within time, but His attributes remain beyond time.
4. Contemplate God's awesomeness!

A Quote to Ponder

"Eternity to the godly is a day that has no sunset; eternity to the wicked is a night that has no sunrise."

Thomas Watson

We Will Live in New Heavens and a New Earth

THE BIG IDEA

God will one day dissolve the present heavens and earth and bring about new heavens and a new earth.

What You Need to Know

- ▶ When Adam and Eve fell, God cursed the earth (Genesis 3:17-18; Romans 8:20-22).

- ▶ Before the eternal kingdom can be made manifest, God must deal with this cursed earth.

- ▶ God will dissolve the present earth and heavens (the atmosphere and the stellar universe) (Psalm 102:25-26; Isaiah 51:6).

- ▶ God will then create new heavens and a new earth (Revelation 21:1-5).

- ▶ Resurrected Christians will thus live in a resurrected universe.

Verses to Contemplate

"The heavens will pass away with a roar" (2 Peter 3:10).

"Then I saw a new heaven and a new earth, for the first heaven and the first earth had passed away" (Revelation 21:1).

FAST FACTS	
The Old Earth	**The New Earth**
tainted by sin and Satan	sin and Satan are gone
decaying—running down	eternal—lasts forever
includes earthly Jerusalem	includes the New Jerusalem

Truths That Transform

1. Scripture reveals that a resurrected people will live in a resurrected universe (Revelation 21:1-5).
2. What happens to our bodies and what happens to the creation go together.
3. The new heavens and earth will be regenerated, free from the curse of sin.

A Quote to Ponder

"Reconcile. Redeem. Restore. Recover. Return. Renew. Regenerate. Resurrect. Each of these biblical words begins with the re- prefix, suggesting a return to an original condition that was ruined or lost."

Randy Alcorn

21

We Will Dwell in the New Jerusalem

THE BIG IDEA

God's eternal city—the New Jerusalem—will rest upon the new earth. Redeemed humans of all ages will eternally inhabit this city.

What You Need to Know

▶ The New Jerusalem—God's eternal city—will rest upon the newly renovated earth (Revelation 21:10).

▶ Redeemed Christians will reside in this city for all eternity (see Revelation 21–22).

▶ It will be a physical city, with gates, streets, and dwelling places (Revelation 21:12).

▶ The city features many jewels and transparent gold, thus allowing God's glory to penetrate it without hindrance (Revelation 21:11,18-21).

Verses to Contemplate

"In my Father's house are many rooms...I go to prepare a place for you" (John 14:2).

"I saw the holy city, new Jerusalem, coming down out of heaven from God" (Revelation 21:2).

FAST FACTS
The Immensity of the New Jerusalem

The city measures 1500 by 1500 by 1500 miles (Revelation 21:16).

This massive height accommodates more than 600,000 stories.

The city will have plenty of room for the redeemed of all ages.

Truths That Transform

1. Finally the purposes of God are fulfilled. God's plan of salvation, conceived in eternity past, is now brought to full fruition (Ephesians 1).
2. Life is everywhere within the eternal city, and death will never intrude again.
3. Light, beauty, holiness, joy, and the presence of God are now abiding realities (Revelation 21:1-5).
4. Set your heart on things above (Colossians 3:1-2).

A Quote to Ponder

"The overall impression of the city as a gigantic brilliant jewel compared to jasper, clear as crystal, indicates its great beauty. John was trying to describe what he saw and to relate it to what might be familiar to his readers. However, it is evident that his revelation transcends anything that can be experienced."

John F. Walvoord

A Famous River and Tree Await Us

THE BIG IDEA

The New Jerusalem will include the river of the water of life and the tree of life, both of which point to abundant spiritual blessings.

What You Need to Know

▶ The "river of the water of life" is a real material river, though it probably also symbolizes the perpetual outflow of spiritual blessing to all the redeemed (Revelation 22:1-2).

▶ The tree of life was last seen in the Garden of Eden in Genesis 3, when Adam and Eve fell into sin and paradise was lost.

▶ Paradise is now gloriously restored, and we again witness the tree of life in the eternal state (Revelation 22:2,14,19).

Verses to Contemplate

"Then the angel showed me the river of the water of life, bright as crystal, flowing from the throne of God and of the Lamb" (Revelation 22:1).

"The tree of life [has] twelve kinds of fruit, yielding its fruit each month" (Revelation 22:2).

FAST FACTS
Healing Leaves on the Tree of Life

The Greek word for "healing" is *therapeia*.

The English word "therapeutic" comes from this word.

The word carries the idea of "health giving."

The tree of life is spiritually health-giving.

Truths That Transform

1. Jesus is our source of living water (John 4:10). He said, "Whoever believes in me, as the Scripture has said, 'Out of his heart will flow rivers of living water'" (John 7:38).
2. Christ guides people in heaven "to springs of living water" (Revelation 7:17).
3. Both in this life and the afterlife, Jesus quenches our spiritual thirst.

A Quote to Ponder

"This ever-flowing river gives a picture of an unending stream of abundant blessings and joy. The tree of life, once banned to guilty humanity (Gen. 3:22-24), will satisfy the city's residents year-round (Rev. 2:7)."

Dennis Johnson

We Will Enjoy Many Activities in Heaven

THE BIG IDEA

You and I will be involved in meaningful and joyful activities throughout all eternity.

What You Need to Know

▶ Service assignments will be entrusted to us in the afterlife according to our degree of faithfulness during our earthly lives (Luke 19:11-26).

▶ We will experience fullness of joy in all our activities (Psalm 16:11).

▶ We will reign with Christ (Revelation 5:10), judge the angels (1 Corinthians 6:3), enjoy fellowship (1 Thessalonians 4:13-17), praise and worship God (Revelation 19:1-6), and explore "the immeasurable riches of his grace" (Ephesians 2:7).

Verses to Contemplate

"Because you have been faithful in a very little, you shall have authority over ten cities" (Luke 19:17).

Redeemed Christians will be "before the throne of God, and serve him day and night" (Revelation 7:15).

We will enjoy fellowship with...

the triune God—Father, Son, and Holy Spirit (Revelation 21:1-5)

Christian family and friends (1 Thessalonians 4:13-17)

biblical personalities, including Abraham, Noah, David, Peter, Paul, and John

Christians of church history, such as Martin Luther and John Calvin

Truths That Transform

1. We will not be playing harps in heaven!
2. Our existence in heaven will be filled with a wide variety of meaningful and joyful activities.
3. Because our service assignments in the afterlife will be determined by our degree of faithfulness during our earthly lives, our wisest course of action is to daily choose to be doers of the Word, not just hearers (James 1:23-25).

A Quote to Ponder

"Faithfulness now is preparation for blessed service then."

Warren Wiersbe

There Will Be No More Sin in Heaven

THE BIG IDEA

All things having to do with sin will be ancient history once we're in the afterlife.

What You Need to Know

- ▶ Sin leads to death (Romans 3:23). But sin and death will be forever absent in heaven.

- ▶ Sin calls for God's wrath (Ephesians 2:3). But God's wrath will be forever absent in heaven. Peace with God will prevail (Romans 5:1).

- ▶ Jesus spoke of sin as blindness (Matthew 23:16-26), bondage (John 8:34), and living in darkness (John 12:35-46). All such things are forever absent in heaven, for sin is absent.

- ▶ Sin led to paradise lost (Genesis 3:23). But heaven is paradise regained (2 Corinthians 12:3; Revelation 2:7), with sin gone forever.

Verses to Contemplate

"I saw the holy city, new Jerusalem, coming down out of heaven from God" (Revelation 21:2; see also 21:10).

"Nothing unclean will ever enter it" (Revelation 21:27).

FAST FACTS
Christ Solved Our Sin Problem

We are forgiven in Christ (Ephesians 1:6-7).

We are justified in Christ (1 Corinthians 6:11).

We are reconciled in Christ (Colossians 1:20).

Truths That Transform

1. In Revelation 21:1-2, heaven is described as "the holy city."
2. There will be no sin or unrighteousness there.
3. This does not mean that you and I must personally attain moral perfection to dwell there. Those who believe in Christ have been given the very righteousness of Christ (see Romans 4:11,22-24).
4. In Christ, we have been made holy (Hebrews 10:14).
5. Rejoice in the salvation Christ has graciously provided for you!

A Quote to Ponder

"We will never sin, never make mistakes, never need to confess...We will never have to defend ourselves, apologize, [or] experience guilt."
Mark Hitchcock

25

Satan Will Be Banned from Heaven

THE BIG IDEA

Satan will be eternally quarantined so that he can no longer attack God or His children.

What You Need to Know

- ▶ Satan's quarantine is a contributing factor to the peace and serene rest we will enjoy in heaven (Revelation 14:13).

- ▶ No longer will Satan be around to promote filth (Matthew 12:24), be our adversary (1 Peter 5:8), propagate lies (John 8:44), and tempt believers (1 Thessalonians 3:5).

- ▶ No longer will Satan counterfeit God's program (2 Corinthians 11:14), promote doctrines of demons (1 Timothy 4:1), and propagate a false gospel (Galatians 1:7-8).

Verses to Contemplate

"Depart from me, you cursed, into the eternal fire prepared for the devil and his angels" (Matthew 25:41).

"The devil who had deceived them was thrown into the

lake of fire and sulfur...and they will be tormented day and night forever and ever" (Revelation 20:10).

Truths That Transform

1. With Satan and demons out of the picture forever—and with sin completely absent—peace, serene rest, and joy become realities.

2. Gone forever will be Satan's solicitations to evil (1 Thessalonians 3:5), his attempts to afflict us with bodily ailments (2 Corinthians 12:7), and the seeds of doubt he seeks to sow in our minds (Genesis 3:4-5).

A Quote to Ponder

"Evil is contagious and must be quarantined...The only way to preserve an eternal place of good is to eternally separate all evil from it. The only way to have an eternal heaven is to have an eternal hell."

Norman Geisler

26

There Will Be No More Death in Heaven

THE BIG IDEA

Once we're in heaven, death and mourning will be gone forever!

What You Need to Know

- ▶ Scripture says that in heaven, death will be swallowed up in victory (1 Corinthians 15:54).

- ▶ This is a Hebrew play on words. Ancient Hebrews believed that death swallowed up the living. But in heaven, things will be reversed—death itself will be swallowed up.

- ▶ Death is part of the old order. In heaven, God says, "Behold, I am making all things new" (Revelation 21:5).

Verses to Contemplate

"He will swallow up death forever; and the Lord GOD will wipe away tears from all faces, and the reproach of his people he will take away from all the earth" (Isaiah 25:8).

"He will wipe away every tear from their eyes, and death

shall be no more, neither shall there be mourning, nor crying, nor pain anymore, for the former things have passed away" (Revelation 21:4).

FAST FACTS
Ancient Jewish Mourning Rituals

Mourning was not an individual matter with private tears.

There was always a very public show of grief, including wailing, putting ashes on the head, and tearing clothes.

Professional mourners were hired to weep and wail.

What a blessed contrast heaven will be!

Truths That Transform

1. Tears, pain, sorrow, and death entered the human race following the fall (Genesis 3).
2. In heaven, the effects of the curse are reversed. Tears, pain, sorrow, and death will be things of the distant past (Revelation 21:4). Life in the eternal city will be painless, tearless, and deathless.

A Quote to Ponder

"How innumerable are the sources of sorrow here; how constant is it on the earth!...How different, therefore, will heaven be when we shall have the assurance that henceforward grief shall be at an end!"

Albert Barnes

27

Many Things Will Be Absent in Heaven

THE BIG IDEA

Many things that we are accustomed to experiencing here on earth will be absent in heaven.

What You Need to Know

- ▶ The sun and moon are not needed for light in the eternal city, for the glory of the Lord will illuminate it (Isaiah 60:19; Revelation 21:23).

- ▶ There is no temple in heaven to which one must go to encounter God, for God's presence will permeate the entire city (Revelation 21:22).

- ▶ There will be no sea in the new earth (Revelation 21:1). There will be an immensely increased land surface for the redeemed.

- ▶ There will be no pain, death, or mourning in heaven. Satan will be banned from heaven (Revelation 20:10; 21:4).

Verses to Contemplate

"The city has no need of sun or moon" (Revelation 21:23).

"I saw no temple in the city" (Revelation 21:22).

"No longer will there be anything accursed" (Revelation 22:3).

Truths That Transform

1. In heaven there will be no more wrongdoing, confession of sin, guilt or shame over any action, or feelings of isolation, loneliness, depression, or discouragement.
2. The absence of negative things will contribute immensely to our sense of joy in heaven.
3. Rejoice in this truth!

A Quote to Ponder

"There shall be no pollution or deformity or offensive defect of any kind, seen in any person or thing; but everyone shall be perfectly pure, and perfectly lovely in heaven."

Jonathan Edwards

28

The Holy Spirit Is Our Heavenly Deposit

THE BIG IDEA

The Holy Spirit within us is a deposit, or guarantee, of what will become ours in the afterlife, including glorious resurrection bodies.

What You Need to Know

- ▶ Paul compared our earthly bodies to tents and our future resurrection bodies to buildings (2 Corinthians 5:1-3).

- ▶ God has given us the Holy Spirit as a guarantee of what is yet to come (2 Corinthians 5:5).

- ▶ The Holy Spirit's presence in our lives guarantees our eventual total transformation and glorification into the likeness of Christ's glorified resurrection body (see Philippians 3:21).

Verses to Contemplate

"He...has given us the Spirit as a guarantee" (2 Corinthians 5:5).

We "were sealed with the promised Holy Spirit, who is the guarantee of our inheritance until we acquire possession of it, to the praise of his glory" (Ephesians 1:13-14).

FAST FACTS
Ministries of the Holy Spirit

The Spirit guides believers (John 16:13), fills and empowers them (Ephesians 5:18), and enables them to overcome sin (Galatians 5:16).

He produces spiritual fruit in believers (Galatians 5:22-23) and bestows spiritual gifts on them (1 Corinthians 12:11).

Truths That Transform

1. Our present bodies are wearing down. They've been infected by a fatal disease—sin. One day, they will simply cease functioning.
2. Our resurrection bodies, by contrast, will never wear down, never get sick, and never die.
3. Count on it! The Holy Spirit in our lives is our guarantee.

A Quote to Ponder

"There will be no blind eyes in heaven. No withered arms or legs in heaven. No pain or agony there. Tears will be gone. Death will be gone. Separation will be gone. This will be the ultimate healing. Then and only then, we will be free at last."

Paul Powell

Let's Anticipate Heaven

THE BIG IDEA

The Bible begins with paradise lost. It ends with paradise regained. Let's live our lives in view of our soon regaining of paradise.

What You Need to Know

▶ Earthly life will soon be over (James 4:14).

▶ Heavenly life is eternal (Revelation 21:1-5).

▶ The incredible glory of the afterlife should motivate each of us to live faithfully during our relatively short time on earth (Romans 8:18).

A Verse to Contemplate

"We look not to the things that are seen but to the things that are unseen. For the things that are seen are transient, but the things that are unseen are eternal" (2 Corinthians 4:18).

A Quote to Ponder

"The God of the universe invites us to view life and death from his eternal vantage point. And if we do, we will see how readily it can revolutionize our lives."

Gary Habermas and J.P. Moreland

Bibliography

Alcorn, Randy. *Heaven*. Wheaton, IL: Tyndale House, 2004.

Baxter, J. Sidlow. *The Other Side of Death*. Grand Rapids, MI: Kregel, 1997.

Baxter, Richard. *Saints' Everlasting Rest*. Philadelphia, PA: Lippincott, 1859.

Boa, Kenneth and Robert Bowman. *Sense and Nonsense about Heaven and Hell*. Grand Rapids, MI: Zondervan, 2007.

Habermas, Gary R. and J.P. Moreland. *Immortality: The Other Side of Death*. Nashville, TN: Nelson, 1992.

Hitchcock, Mark. *55 Answers to Questions About Life After Death*. Sisters, OR: Multnomah Books, 2005.

Lotz, Anne Graham. *Heaven: My Father's House*. Nashville, TN: Nelson, 2001.

MacArthur, John. *The Glories of Heaven*. Wheaton, IL: Crossway Books, 1996.

Pache, Rene. *The Future Life*. Chicago, IL: Moody, 1980.

Ryle, J.C. *Heaven*. Great Britain: Christian Focus, 2001.

Sanders, J. Oswald. *Heaven: Better by Far*. Grand Rapids, MI: Discovery House, 1993.

Smith, Wilbur M. *The Biblical Doctrine of Heaven*. Chicago, IL: Moody, 1974.

Tada, Joni Eareckson. *Heaven: Your Real Home*. Grand Rapids, MI: Zondervan, 1995.

To learn more about Harvest House books and
to read sample chapters, log on to our website:

www.harvesthousepublishers.com

HARVEST HOUSE PUBLISHERS
EUGENE, OREGON